BRITAIN IN PICTURES
THE BRITISH PEOPLE IN PICTURES

THE ENGLISH BIBLE

GENERAL EDITOR
W. J. TURNER

The Editor is most grateful to all those who have
so kindly helped in the selection of illustrations
especially to officials of the various public
Museums Libraries and Galleries and
to all others who have generously
allowed pictures and MSS
to be reproduced

THE ENGLISH BIBLE

SIR HERBERT GRIERSON

WITH
8 PLATES IN COLOUR
AND
21 ILLUSTRATIONS IN
BLACK & WHITE

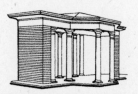

WILLIAM COLLINS OF LONDON
MCMXXXXIII

PRODUCED BY
ADPRINT LIMITED LONDON

SECOND IMPRESSION

PRINTED IN GREAT BRITAIN BY
CLARKE & SHERWELL LTD NORTHAMPTON
ON MELLOTEX BOOK PAPER MADE BY
TULLIS RUSSELL & CO LTD MARKINCH SCOTLAND

LIST OF ILLUSTRATIONS

PLATES IN COLOUR

BLACK AND WHITE ILLUSTRATIONS

A BRIEF GENEALOGY OF THE ENGLISH BIBLE

1. The *Septuagint* : Greek translation of the Old Testament Scriptures made from the Hebrew and Aramaic for the Jews in dispersion, 3rd century B.C.—c.2nd century A.D.

2. The so-called *Vulgate* : a revision by St. Jerome (c. 340-420) of the Old Latin version ; New Testament and Psalter translated from the Greek ; the rest of the O.T. translated from Hebrew and (Book of Daniel and Apocrypha) from Aramaic or Chaldee.

3. English Wycliffe or *Lollard* version of the *Vulgate*. 14th century.

4. Hebrew Bible or O.T., which was to displace the Greek and Latin in the 16th century, so-called *Massoretic* text ; complete version printed at Brescia, 1494, and used by Luther whose influence was felt by all English translators.

5. Erasmus's text of the N.T., with Latin translation and copious notes, issued 1516, *et seq.*

6. Luther's German translation : O.T. from Hebrew, N.T. from Erasmus's text, 1522.

7. Tyndale's English N.T., 1528, 1534, 1535, based on Erasmus's texts (2nd and 3rd editions of 1519, 1522) with aid from Luther's version and *Vulgate* ; Pentateuch, 1530; Book of Jonah, 1531, from Hebrew.

8. Miles Coverdale's complete translation of the Bible from the *Vulgate* and Luther's version, 1535.

9. Matthew's Bible, "the foundation of all the later English versions," derived mainly from Tyndale and Coverdale, 1537.

10. Cromwell's Bible, April 1539 ; Cranmer's Bible, April 1540, revised November 1540. These constituted the *Great Bible* read in Churches.

11. *Geneva Bible*, "translated according to the Ebrue and Greeke," 1560.

12. *The Bishop's Bible*, 1568; with revision, 1572. Official basis of :

13. *Authorised Version*, 1611.

14. *Revised Version*, "being the version set forth, A.D. 1611, compared with the most ancient authorities and revised." N.T., 1881. O.T. and N.T. together, 1885.

15. More modern versions are : *Twentieth Century New Testament*, based on Westcott and Hort, 1901, revised 1904 ; Weymouth's *New Testament in Modern Speech*, 1902 ; Moulton's *Modern Reader's Bible*, 1907 ; Moffatt's *New Translation*, 1913.

THE TRANSLATORS: WYCLIF TO MOFFATT

VERY sort of doctrine which is to be delivered to the faithful," says the Catechism of the Council of Trent, "is contained in the Word of God, which is divided into Scripture and Tradition." And the Scripture had always, at least in theory, held the first place. In his exposition and defence of Christian doctrine Thomas Aquinas has two courts of appeal,—firstly Scripture, and secondly "the Philosopher," that is Aristotle, in matters scientific, but the latter is subject to correction by the former. The Scriptures were represented, for those who could read, by the Vulgate, St. Jerome's Latin translation of the Old and New Testament. The rhythm of the English Bible, as that finally emerged, owes not a little to the Latin of St. Jerome, though Tyndale will assert that both Hebrew and Greek are more easily rendered into English than into Latin.

The influence of the Scriptures, Old and New Testament, on English literature goes back to the earliest extant records of that literature—the Caedmonian poetic version of the books of *Genesis* and *Exodus* and of the apocryphal *Judith* (which in the Vulgate is included among the historical books) followed later by the *Crist* of Cynewulf, a noble poem. Just before his death the Venerable Bede was engaged on a translation of the Gospel of St. John, and the last work of King Alfred was a translation of the Psalter. If from the date of the Norman Conquest to the fourteenth century there were fewer English versions of Biblical literature that was because English was the language of a conquered people. Those who could read at all could also read Latin and French. Yet in many ways the main story of the Old and New Testament was made familiar to the people. The *Ormulum*, our oldest poem in a regular syllabic metre, is an exposition of the Gospels for each day. There were poetical paraphrases of *Genesis* and *Exodus*, and the *Cursor Mundi* told in rude accentual verse a history of the world, including the main episodes which were made familiar to the people in the popular Miracle Plays. The great English mystic of the fourteenth century, Richard Rolle of Hampole, made two prose versions of the Psalms with commentaries, as well as extracts from the Books of Job and Jeremiah. The didactic alliterative poem *Piers Plowman* is pervaded with the Spirit of the Bible and enforces its teaching with excerpts from the Vulgate. Caxton in his translation of the *Golden Legend* included stories from the Old Testament. The general story of the Bible was fairly well known in the fourteenth century; but "save for the Psalms, of all that is not story, notably the Prophets in the Old Testament and the Epistles in the New, there was small opportunity for any one ignorant of Latin to gain knowledge, and this was the case also with the whole Bible in respect of its text as distinct from its general purport." (Pollard.)

It was with the first stirrings of reform, the revolt against the corruptions of the Mediaeval Church (and one may confine the word to corruptions which the Roman Church admitted and in great part set itself to correct later) that a new importance began to be attached to the Bible, a movement which might, without irreverence, be described as Swift does in the *Tale of a Tub*, as a determination to see if the Will was being faithfully observed. We sometimes hear it suggested that it was the translation of the Scriptures that led to the Reformation. It might be more justly said that the Reformation led to a renewed and closer study of the Scriptures. The Church, at least in its higher orders, but in all to some extent, had like Jeshurun waxed fat and kicked, with results that were felt in all ranks of society from the king upon his throne to the peasant preyed upon by friars and summoners and pardoners. "Everything," as a Commission of 1537 reported to the Pope, "could be obtained for money, however hurtful it might be to the general welfare of the Church." Moreover, what has been said above, that those who could read could also read Latin and French, must be qualified by the fact that not many, even of the clergy, could understand Latin, even the Latin of the services which they read.

The translation of the Bible into English was thus coincident with, and a consequence of, a revolt against the practices, and in the wake of that against the dogmas, of the Catholic Church, an attitude which was, as we shall see, often emphasised by the glosses which accompanied the translation. In estimating, therefore, the influence of the Bible on our people and literature there are two things to be kept in mind : firstly, the purely literary effect of possessing in the vernacular such a magnificent body of literature, narrative and poetic—for the prophetic is also the poetic

8

Ere to fore we haue made mencion of occupacion of thumayne lygnage which durith fro Septuagesme vnto Ester / here after we shal make mencion of the tyme of reconsiliacion / which durith fro Ester vnto the vtas of whitsontyde / lyke as holy chyrche hath ordeyned /

The Resurrection of our lord Jhesu cryst was the thirde day after his deth / And of this blessyd resurreccion / seuen thynges ben to be consydered / Fyrst of the tyme that he was in the sepulcre / that he thre dayes and thre nyghtes he was in the sepulcre / And the thirde day he arose Secondly wherfore he arose not anon whan he was deed / But abode vnto the thirde day / Thirdely how he arose / Fourthly wherfor his resurreccion taryed not vntyl the generall resurreccion / Fyftly wherfore he arose / Sixtly how ofte tymes he appered in his resurreccion / And the seuenth / how the holy faders which were enclosed in a partye of helle / he delyuerd / what he dyd as to the first poynt / it ought to be knowen that Jhesus was in the sepulcre iij dayes and iij nyghtes / But after saynt austyn the first day is taken by synodocle / that is that the last part of the day is taken

The secod day is take all hool / the third is taken after the first part of the day / thus ther be iij dayes / and euery day hath his nyght goyng byfore / and after toke the ordre of þe dayes was chaunged and þe cours ordeyned / for byfore / þ dayes wente byfore / and the nyghtes folowed / after the tyme of the passyd / that ordre was chaunged / for the nyghtes god by þ fore and this is by mysterie / For man first ouerthrewe in the day / and fyll in to the nyght of synne / And by the passyon and resurreccion of Jhesu cryst he can agayn fro the nyght of synne vnto þ day of grace / As touchyng the secod consideracion / if ought to be knowen / þ it is accordynge to reson that and after his deth he ought not to aryse / But ought to abyde vnto þ thirde day / and that for .ij. resos / the first for the signyfycacion / to that / that the lyght of his deth shold cure our double deth / and therfore .j. day hool and ij nyghtes he laye in sepulcre / that by the day we vnderstande the light of his deth / and by the ij nyghtes our double deth / and this

THE RESURRECTION

Page from Caxton's *Golden Legend*, 1483

By courtesy of Corpus Christi College, Cambridge

WILLIAM TYNDALE 1492–1536

Oil painting by an unknown artist

By courtesy of the Principal and Fellows of Hertford College, Oxford

whether one thinks of Isaiah or St. Paul: secondly, the effect on the mind of the English people, represented by some prominent figures in our literature, of the acceptance of this literature, rich in narrative and poetry but entirely devoid of science, as the inspired Word of God, all in that respect on the same, or practically the same, level.

The new approach to the Bible began with the first complete translation, the Wyclifite or Lollard Bible of the fourteenth century, for to Wyclif the Bible was not only the ultimate but the only authority on matters of religious belief and practice : and to this he added the other doctrine fundamental to Protestantism, the right of every man, learned or ignorant, to examine the Bible for himself.

The Lollard Bible is not now thought to be the work of Wyclif himself. Wyclif's own versions are rather to be found in his homilies, where, if the homily were removed, we should have a valuable and fairly continuous translation of the New Testament. "In one set of *Epistolae Dominicales* Wyclif expressly states that his motive was to tell in English Paul's Epistles." (Workman : *Life of Wyclif.*) The Bible has come down to us in, for the greater part of it, two versions, both of course from the Vulgate; the time for Greek and Hebrew was not yet come. The first of these is attributed to a Nicholas Hereford, one of Wyclif's supporters at Oxford; the other, on less probable grounds, to a John Purvey, another friend of the reformer. The interest of this second version is that the translator, whom we may call Purvey, breaks away from the too literal rendering of Latin idiom in the direction which Tyndale was to follow, the acceptance of the native English idiom and order of words, the use even of colloquial expressions. Purvey, who describes himself as "on symple creature of God," explains among many other things, in a long, interesting, and very Wyclifite, prologue, in what various ways a translator may deal with different Latin idioms, such as *e.g.* the ablative absolute.

The Lollard Heresy was suppressed on the accession to the throne of Henry IV, the son of that John of Gaunt who, for political purposes, had been a supporter of Wyclif against the prelates. It was suppressed, but not annihilated, by the passing of the act *De Heretico Comburendo* and the persecution which ensued. The Lollard Bible circulated continuously, as is proved by the survival of some hundred and eighty manuscripts ; and it kept alive the temper which accepted the Bible as the sole and supreme authority in religion, a spirit which reasserted itself so soon as the influence of the new heresy of Luther began to flow in from the Continent. It was in this spirit that the work of translation was resumed in the sixteenth century. Meantime the Renaissance had come. Hebrew and Greek had to be reckoned with. The Vulgate was being subjected to criticism. Erasmus published a Greek text of the New Testament in 1516, and a Latin translation in 1519 ; and it was from Erasmus's text that Luther made his German translation which was published in September 1522.

9

The hero and martyr of the English Bible as we have it is William Tyndale (or Hutchins), born about 1494 and educated at Oxford and Cambridge, where, especially at the latter, he came in contact with the new learning and acquired an impatience with the old, and with the restrictions attached to a knowledge of the genuine Scriptures. As a tutor in a family in the Cotswolds he continued his studies and translated both the *Enchiridion Militis Christiani* of Erasmus and, from the Greek, a speech of Isocrates. When finally, provoked by the ignorance of the clergy whom he met at his master's table, and by accusations of heresy, he resolved to "cause a boy that driveth the plough" to know more of the scripture than they, and went to London to seek the patronage of the Bishop of London, Cuthbert Tunstall, he took the latter translation with him as a proof of his competence. But he found that neither London nor England was a safe place for such a task, and he went to Germany. Settling at Cologne, with a rather talkative and troublesome colleague, William Roye, he began to prepare a quarto edition of the New Testament with a prologue and very Lutheran glosses. What was being prepared was discovered by an English spy, and Tyndale fled to Worms, where he issued a complete translation, but without prologue or glosses, in octavo form, about February 1526. Of this early edition three copies survive. A carefully revised edition was issued by Tyndale in 1534 with prefaces general and special, references, glosses, and including the epistles taken from the Old Testament and the Apocrypha as used in the service-book of Salisbury. A further edition, slightly revised, was published in 1535, Tyndale's final text. But in the interval between the completion of the first New Testament and this latter year he had been busy with the Old Testament, and in 1530 printed his version of the *Pentateuch* in 1530 and of *Jonah* in 1531. In 1535 he was seized by treachery, imprisoned in the castle of Vilvorde and a year later "he was brought forth to the place of execution, was there tied to the stake, and then strangled first by the hangman, and afterwards with fire consumed . . . crying thus at the stake with a fervent zeal and a loud voice : Lord, open the King of England's eyes." (Foxe.) His chief opponent in controversy, Sir Thomas More, had suffered a similar fate a year earlier.

Of Tyndale's version I shall shortly print an extract or two beside those of later ones with a view to show how the one led on to the others, and what a composite piece of work the Authorised version of 1611 is. But there are some features of Tyndale's work which it is only fair to indicate at once, for his sake and for that of his opponents, such as Sir Thomas More ; for Tyndale's sake, because the later changes were not all for the better. His is the racier style if it includes some questionable devices, as varying the word by which one word in the original is rendered, and using contemporary words not always applicable : "We sailed away from Philippos after the ester holydays" (Acts xx. 6.); "on a Sondaye" (Rev. i. 10.). But

'The Martyrdome of Master William Tindall in Flanders by Vilvord Castle'
Engraving from Foxe's *Acts and Monuments of Martyrs*, 1684

how racy and colloquial are such phrases as : "Then said the serpent unto the woman: 'Tush ye shall not die,'" "And the Lord was with Joseph and he was a lucky fellow," "When ye pray bable not much," "a void ground and a roaring wilderness," (The "howling wilderness" of the Authorised has become common usage.) and many others. To Tyndale we owe the word "Jehovah" to which we are now taught to prefer the barbaric "Javeh." To him also we owe some fine Hebraisms : "To die the death," "in the sweat of thy face," "the living God," "sick unto death," "uncircumcised lips."

Against all this and more must be set, from a Catholic point of view, his use of tendencious forms as "congregation" for "Church," "senior" and later "elder" to translate "presbuteros" rather than "priest" which was kept for "hiereus," "repentance" for "penance," etc. More justifiable was the complaint of Tyndale's tendencious notes. Some are simply doctrinal, Calvinistic, as the note at the beginning of the benedictions (Matth. v.) intended to correct any thought of human merit : "All these

deeds here rehearsed, as to nourish peace, to shew mercy, to suffer persecution and so forth, make not a man happy and blessed, neither deserve
reward of heaven: but declare and testify that we are happy and blessed, and
that we shall have great promotion in heaven, and certify us in our hearts
that we are God's sons, that the Holy Ghost is in us, for all good things
are given to us freely of God for Christ's blood's sake and his merits."
Others, which a modern critic describes as "amusing," were to a Catholic
very offensive : "How shall I curse whom God curseth not" ("The pope
can tell how"). "Neither bring the hire of a whore nor the price of a dog
in to the house of the Lord thy God" ("The pope will take tribute of them
yet, and bishops, and abbots desire no better tenants"). "And they
blessed Rebecca" ("to bless a man's neighbour is to pray for him, and to
wish him good : not to wag two fingers over him"). "They shall make
them no baldness upon their heads" ("Of the heathen priests therefore
took our prelates the ensample of their bald pates"). "And these words
which I command thee this day shall be in thine heart, and thou shalt
whet them on thy children, and shalt talk of them at home in thine house
&c." ("It is heresy with us for a lay man to look of God's Word or to read
it"). "And he [Joseph] appointed the people, unto the cities, from one side
of Egypt unto the other, only the land of priests bought he not. For there
was an ordinance made by Pharaoh for the priests, etc." ("The blind guides
get privileges from bearing with their brethren, contrary to Christ's law
of love. And of these priests of idols did our compassing ivytrees learn
to creep up little by little and to compass the great trees of the world with
hypocrisy, and·to thrust the roots of idolatrous superstition in to them
and to suck out the juice of them with their poetry, till all be seer boughs
and no thing green save their own commonwealth"). "Ye shall put nothing
unto the word which I command you neither do aught there from etc."
("No ; nor yet corrupt it with false glosses to confirm Aristotle's false
lerning therwith"). The last note shows Tyndale's sympathy with the new
learning which was in revolt against Aristotle. But it is little wonder
that Sir Thomas More distrusted a translation animated by such a spirit.
On the other hand it must be remembered that behind Tyndale's passionate
notes lay a century of persecution and burnings.

Meantime another pioneer of translation, Miles Coverdale, no scholar
such as Tyndale, nor with the same racy and vigorous style, but master
of a pleasing and readable English, had made a complete translation
which he described as "faithfully and truly translated out of Douche
and Latin," that is from the Vulgate and Luther. The reference to Luther
was soon dropped. This was published in 1535 with an unauthorised
dedication to the King : "Josias commanded straitly (as your grace doth)
that the law of God should be read and taught unto all the people."
It was probably printed at Zurich, and is the first complete Bible in English
and the first entirely by one man. Coverdale has some interesting

'The Miraculous Draught of Fishes'
Woodcut from Tyndale's Bible. St. Luke, chapter 5.

renderings of his own. I quote from Mr. Isaac's chapter in *Ancient English Versions of the Bible* (1940) not having Coverdale's at hand. In the sections of which his is the first modern translation: Jer. viii. 22, "There is no more triacle at Galaad"; Ps. xc. 5, "Thou shalt not need to be afraid for eny bugges by night"; Isa. xxiv. 9, "the beer shal be byter to them that drinke it" etc. Coverdale's version was followed in 1537 by what is known as Matthew's Bible. This was (for Henry had now broken definitely with the Pope and declared himself Supreme Head of the Church) issued "with the Kinge's most gracyous lycence" and is therefore our first Authorised version. It is a composite Bible,—Tyndale's Pentateuch and New Testament, Coverdale's Apocrypha and version of Ezra to Malachi, and a new version of Joshua to Chronicles now believed to be that left by Tyndale in manuscript. It is from the Hebrew and has all his peculiarities, as the varying of the word to render the same word in the original. But the whole book has been edited by one John Rogers or so it is generally accepted, a competent editor whoever he was. On these were based the so called Great Bibles including Cromwell's 1539, Cranmer's (he having contributed a prologue) 1540, and the King's. This was the Bible appointed to be used in Churches. It was revised with each issue; but more popular and more important for later versions was the Geneva Bible, the New Testament issued in 1557, the Psalms in 1559, and the Bible in 1560 with a dedication to the Queen, Elizabeth. This is known sometimes as the Breeches Bible because of the verse in Genesis: "and they sowed figge leaves together and made themselves breeches." Tyndale's word had been "apurns" to which the Authorised reverted as "aprons." Tyndale's spelling is interesting for the pronunciation of the time. He always spells "childeren" and "bretheren"; and "childern" was Milton's spelling in the first edition of *Paradise Lost*.

The Geneva Bible was the work of Protestant refugees from the Marian persecution, especially William Whittington, a fellow of All Souls College, Oxford. The New Testament is based on Tyndale, the Old on the Great Bible; but the work was done with a scholarly regard to the Hebrew and Greek and there are divergencies from the Tyndale-Coverdale tradition, some of which have found their way into the Authorized text. All these later versions, from Matthew's onwards, owe a good deal to the French translations of Lefevre (1534) and Olivetan (1535). To the Geneva Bible in its first edition was prefixed a prologue by Calvin; and the translation is accompanied from the first verse to the last with a running commentary in marginal glosses. So far as the present writer can judge from some study of them in very small print in a copy of 1610, these are not so pointedly savage as those of Tyndale. The worst of the fight was over. But all the contents of the Apocalypse are interpreted as applying to the Church of Rome. Some of the glosses seem sensible and humane: "And they called Rebecca and said unto her, Wilt thou go with this man?" ("This showeth that parents have not authoritie to marry their children without consent of the parties.") "I demand then, hath God cast away his people? God forbid, etc." ("Now the Apostle sheweth how this doctrine is to be applied to others abiding still in his propounded case. Therefore he teacheth us that all the Jews are not cast away, and therefore we ought not to pronounce rashly of private persons whether they be of the number of the elect or not, etc.")

This was the popular Bible, that read by Shakespeare for example, though the Great Bible was that read in Church. Between the Geneva and the Authorised of 1611 there came one more revision of the Great Bible, the so-called Bishop's Bible issued in 1568, and with some revision in 1572. It has been described as "a backward looking Bible usually ignoring the improvements in music and accuracy of the Geneva version in favour of the traditional readings of the Great Bible." (*The Bible in its Ancient and English Versions*. Edited by H. Wheeler Robinson, 1940.) But it does not always follow either. In the Psalms especially, so far as the present writer has examined them, it has often a text of its own of a not very attractive character musically. Nevertheless it is the source, the issue of 1572, of several phrases familiar to us from the Authorised: "the voice of one crying in the wilderness," "less than the least of all

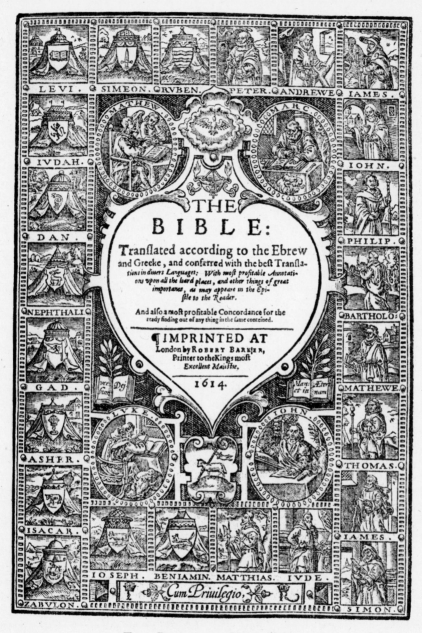

THE
BIBLE:
Translated according to the Ebrew
and Greeke, and conferred with the best Translations in diuers Languages: With most profitable Annotati-
ons vpon all the hard places, and other things of great
importance, as may appeare in the Epi-
stle to the Reader.

And also a most profitable Concordance for the
ready finding out of any thing in the same conteined.

❧IMPRINTED AT
London by ROBERT BARKER,
Printer to the Kings most
Excellent Maiestie.
1614.

Titles in border (clockwise from top left): LEVI. SIMEON. RVBEN. PETER. ANDREWE. IAMES. IOHN. PHILIP. BARTHOLO: MATHEWE. THOMAS. IAMES. SIMON. IVDE. MATTHIAS. BENIAMIN. IOSEPH. ZABVLON. ISACAR. ASHER. GAD. NEPHTHALI. DAN. IVDAH. MATHEW. MARC. LVKE. IOHN.

Cum Priuilegio.

TITLE PAGE OF THE GENEVA BIBLE
English reprint of 1614

saints" (for ἐμοὶ τῷ ἐλαχιστοτέρῳ παντων ἁγίων), "Rend your hearts and not your garments" and some others.

It was on the one hand the feeling that the Geneva Bible was a better translation than any of the Great Bibles, and on the other the dislike of many, including King James, for the tendencious glosses, that led to the resolve, at the Hampton Court Conference, to prepare yet another version. Three committees were appointed, for Oxford, Cambridge and Westminster, and the work divided among them. Instructions were issued of which only one or two need be cited : the Bishop's Bible (1572) was to be followed as closely as possible. The older ecclesiastical words were to be kept instead of Tyndale's innovations ; there were to be no marginal glosses except to explain some Hebrew or Greek word. Tyndale remains the hero of the English Bible. His rendering was the raciest. All that is best in the final version of the New Testament derives from Tyndale. It is regrettable that his text of 1535 is accessible only in the rather heavy Hexapla of Bagster.

The Roman Catholic version known as the Douay Bible, of which the New Testament appeared at Rheims in 1582, the Old Testament at Douai in 1609-10, lies a little out of the main current but was consulted by the revisers. It is from the Vulgate, and the translators retained the technical terms in their original form ; "Pasch" (passover), but also "make the phase" (keep the passover) ; "loaves of proposition" (shew bread) ; "scenopegia" (feast of tabernacles) etc. A number of Latin words are also retained from the Vulgate as "inquination," "potestates," "longanimity" (which may explain its frequent use by Donne). But none of these peculiarities has found its way into the language. It is more interesting to note the claim in the introduction that the Latin of the Vulgate is based on older Hebrew texts than those available in the sixteenth century. This is quite true. All the extant Hebrew texts of the Old Testament derive from one and the same source. But St. Jerome may have known older manuscripts or Jewish traditional readings, and the Greek Bible known as the Septuagint "was made from the Hebrew text over a thousand years before the date of the earliest existing copy of the Hebrew text." (David Daiches : *The King James Version of the Bible*, 1941.) These are important facts for revision, at any time, of the text ; not for the history of the English Bible and its influence.

The revision of the Authorised Version of 1611 in the nineteenth century was the outcome of a growing body of criticism which is summarised by Professor Cadoux : "Not only had successive printers introduced into it [the Authorised] numerous small alterations, so that there was no fixed standard for its wording, but it was replete with increasingly obscure archaisms and—what was worse—inconsistencies and errors innumerable, which the progress of scholarship was rendering more and more intolerable. Nor indeed was it free from the dogmatic bias to which

JAMES I
The King responsible for the Authorised Version of 1611
Oil painting by Paul van Somer, 1576-1621

different groups of its translators had been (perhaps in part unconsciously) subject." (Robinson, *op. cit.*) The work began in 1870, separate committees being appointed for the Old and the New Testament. The New Testament was issued in 1881, the Old and New together in May 1885. The translation was rather savagely attacked by Dr. Burgon, Dean of Chichester, and others including the late Professor Saintsbury in his *History of English Prose Rhythm*, his fine ear jarred by the changes in old and familiar cadences. It is not for the present writer to enter into a now old controversy. There can be no doubt that for certain of the books of the Old Testament, as the *Book of Job* and the Prophets generally, a study of the Revised version is indispensable by anyone interested in the meaning as well as the rhythm. Nor should the marginal readings be overlooked. But the main theme of the present volume is the Bible in England in the hey-day of its acceptance as the entire and unchallenged Word of God.

But the Revised version was an experiment, or more truly a double experiment, firstly to alter the Elizabethan English just sufficiently to secure accuracy and clearness; and secondly to correct the Authorised so far as seemed essential in the light of advanced Hebrew and Greek scholarship. In both respects the result was a compromise, especially as regards the latter aim. The Masoretic text of the Hebrew Scriptures is in places, Dr. Moffatt declares, very corrupt. The text of the New Testament adopted by the translators is not thought to be so trustworthy as that which was being worked out by Westcott and Hort. The present writer is not qualified to discuss these questions, nor is this the place to attempt any such estimate. He records the opinion of scholars to explain why the work of the revisers was soon followed by various attempts to go further in both directions, a closer approximation to modern English, a bolder treatment of the original source, Hebrew and Greek. The best known and most revolutionary is that of Dr. James Moffatt, late of the Theological Seminary, New York. The New Testament appeared in 1913, the Old Testament in 1924, the complete Bible in 1926, and revised in 1935.

Moffatt's English is colloquial and familiar with frequent clichés. Admitting his scholarship to be sound, one gets often the sense of passages formerly found obscure, and for certain books, as the Epistles of St. Paul, he does provide a more intelligible text. This is probably also true of the difficult prophetic books, which, too, he boldly breaks up in accordance with the dating and dividing of scholars, which must be conjectural in character. Poetically to one familiar with the older versions there is undoubtedly loss or apparent loss. It is just a question how far such an experiment as Moffatt's here or Lawrence's in the *Odyssey* can be successful. At times, too, some overfamiliarity or unhappy association produces a reading which jars badly, *e.g.* Matthew xxvi. 34.

The New Testament in Basic English, 1941, is an experiment in using a limited range of language, avoiding synonyms at all costs. For this particular work one thousand words was allowed in place of the usual eight hundred and fifty of the official Basic English vocabulary. The rendering is not wanting in dignity. There are fewer clichés than in Moffatt's. But the disadvantage is that, when there are apparently several synonyms, there are generally different shades of meaning and one may lose by adhering to the same word or phrase throughout. "One of you will be false to me," "Judas who was false to him." There are more ways of being false to a friend than actually betraying him to his mortal foes. Similarly there are more ways of being "untrue in married life" than actually committing adultery.

It is strange at first sight that Scotland, which accepted so completely the Reformation as that came to it from Geneva, failed to secure a version of the Scriptures in the vernacular. Under Knox, Scotland accepted the Genevan version; and later the authorised Jacobean Bible. The use of an English version of the Scriptures and the currency of Knox's controversial pamphlets "were the most effective agents . . . in undermining the position of the Scots tongue as a literary dialect." (J. H. Millar: *A Literary History of Scotland*).

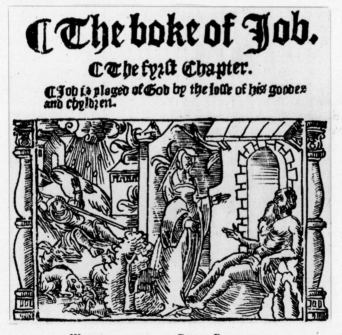

WOODCUT FROM THE GREAT BIBLE, 1539

EFORE going into any detail as to the influence of the English Bible as literature I propose to give in consecutive order short extracts from the various versions, the same passage or passages in the Lollard, in Tyndale, in the Geneva version and in the Authorised : but it might be well to begin with the Vulgate :

"Si linguis hominum loquar et angelorum, critatem autem non habeam, factus sum velut aes sonans, aut cymbalum tinniens. Et si habuero prophetiam, et noverim mysteria omnia, et omnem scientiam ; et si habuero omnem fidem ita ut montes transferam, caritatem autem non habuero, nihil sum. Et si distribuero in cibos pauperum omnes facultates meas, et si tradiderim corpus meum ita ut ardeam, caritatem autem non habuero, nihil mihi prodest . . . Nunc autem manent, fides, spes, caritas, tria haec ; major autem horum est caritas."

This is the immediate source of the Lollard rendering :

"If I speke with tonges of men and angels, and I have not charite, I am made as bras sowninge or a cymbal tinklynge, and if I have profecie, and know alle mysteries, and al kynninge, and if I have al feith so that I meve hills fro her place, and I have not charite I am nought, and if I departe alle my godis into metis of pore men, and if I bitake my bodi so that I brenne, and I have not charite it profiteth me no thing . . . and now dwellen feith hope and charite ; but the most of these is charite."

Tyndale's version follows in which it will be noticed he uses the past subjunctive for the present in both Greek and Latin, probably to heighten the hypothetical cast of the statement :

"Though I spake with the tonges of men and angels and yet had not love I were even as sounding brass or as a tynklynge Cymball. And though I coude prophesy and understode all secretes and all knowledge : yea if I hade all fayth so that I coude move mountaynes oute of ther places and yet had no love I were nothynge. And though I bestowed al my goodes to fede the poore ; and though I gave my body even that I burned and yet had no love, it profiteth me nothing . . . Now abydeth fayth hope love even these three but the chief of these is love."

Tyndale changes "charity" to "love" for the Greek "agape." There are two Greek words, *agape* and *eros*, the latter the love of passion. But the English "charity" has also acquired misleading implications. The Geneva version runs :

"Though I speake with the tongues of men and Angels, and have not love, I am as sounding brasse or a tinkling cymball. And though I had the *gift* of prophesie, and knew all secrets and all knowledge, yea, if I had al faith, so that I could remove mountains, and had not love, I were nothing. And though

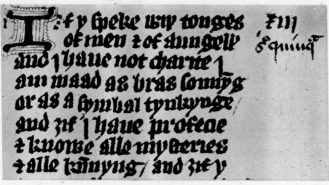

I feede the poore with all my goodes, and though I give my body; that I bee burned, and have not love, it profiteth mee nothing . . . And now abideth faith, hope, and love, *even* these three ; but the chiefest of these is love."

Here the present and past interchange. Here too begins the custom of printing in italics any words added for the sense. Finally here are the Authorised and Revised versions :

"Though I speak with the tongues of men and of angels and have not charity, I am become *as* sounding brass or a tinkling cymbal. And though I have *the gift of* prophesy, and understand all mysteries, and all knowledge ; and though I have all faith, so that I could remove mountains, and have not charity, I am nothing. And though I bestow all my goods to feed *the poor*, and though I give my body to be burned, and have not charity, it profiteth me nothing . . And now abideth faith, hope, and charity, these three ; but the greatest of these is charity."

Notice "the most," "the chief," "the chiefest," "the gretest." The principal changes made in the Revised version, which I need not print at length, were "love" for "charity," a reversion to Tyndale, and "clanging" for "tinkling." The former provoked much protest.

Of the Prophets the version till the Authorised of 1611 had been in the main Coverdale's, and it may be well to take a short extract from the Lollard version and Coverdale's, giving the Vulgate version first for comparison again with that of the later text—the beautiful verses which close the fortieth chapter of Isaiah :

"Numquid nescis, aut non audisti : Deus sempiternus Dominus, qui creavit terminos terrae, non deficiet, neque laborabit, nec est investigatio sapientiae ejus ? Qui dat lasso virtutem, et his qui non sunt fortitudinem et robur multiplicat. Deficient pueri, et laborabunt, et juvenes in infirmatate cadent. Qui

21

autem sperant in Domino mutabunt fortitudinem, assument pennas sicut aquilae, current et non laborabunt, ambulabunt et non deficient."

Purvey's version of this runs:

"Whether thou knowest not, ether herdest thou not ? God everlasting Lord, that made of nouht the endis of erthe, schal not faile, nether schal travele, nether enserching of his wisdom is : That gyreth vertu to the weeri, and strength to hem that ben not, and multiplieth stalworthnesse. Children schulen faile, and schulen travele, and yonge men schullen falle doun in her sicknesse. But thei that hopen in the Lord schulen chaunge strengthe, thei schulen take fetheris as eglis : thei schulen renne and schulen not travele, thei schulen go, and schulen not faile."

Coverdale's, as it stands in Matthew's Bible and again in the Great Bible of 1539, runs :

"Knowest thou not, or hast thou not hearde, that the everlasting God, the Lorde which made all the corners of the earth, is nether weery nor faynt ? and that his wysdom cannot be comprehended : but that he geveth strength unto the weery and power unto the faynte ? Children are weery and faynt, and the strongest men fall : But unto them that have the Lord before theyr eyes shal strength be encreased. Aegles winges shal grow upon them : when they runne, they shall not fall ; and when they go they shall not be weery."

It is with some help from the Genevan that the Authorised achieves its magnificent rendering :

"Hast thou not known ? Hast thou not heard, *that* the everlasting God, the Lord, the Creator of the ends of the earth, fainteth not, neither is weary ? There is no searching of his understanding. He giveth power to the faint ; and to *them that have* no might he increaseth strength. Even the youths shall faint and be weary, and the young men shall utterly fall. But they that wait upon the Lord shall renew *their* strength ; they shall mount up with wings as eagles ; they shall run and not be weary ; *and* they shall walk, and not faint."

The Revised version of 1884 reads for "them that have" "him that hath." But Coverdale's great achievement was his version of the Psalter which is still used in the Anglican Prayer Book. That final version was the result of a good deal of revision. The text of Coverdale's own Bible and of Matthew's Bible is not quite that of 1539 which is the Prayer Book's text. The changes are often small but occasionally considerable, *e.g.* in the well known twenty-third : "The Lord is my shepherd."

What then is to be said of the influence of the English Bible on our own prose and verse ? Some things must be set aside as erroneous. It is, I think, Mr. Somerset Maugham who in a recent volume lays it to the charge of our reading the Bible so much that we acquired the ideal of prose represented by Dr. Johnson and Gibbon, which is absurd. The prose of the Bible, it has often been pointed out, is not the prose of the century in which the final version was made, the period of Hooker and Bacon and Milton and Browne. That ideal had another source, in Latin

Though I spake with the tonges of men and aungels, and haue no loue, I am euen as soundyng brasse: or as a tynklynge cymball. And though I coulde prophesy, and vnderstande al secretes, and all knowledge: pea, yf I had a* all fayth, so that I could moue moūtayns out of their places, and yet had no loue, I were nothynge. And though I bestowe all my goodes (to fede the poore) and though I gyue my body euen that I burned, and yet haue no loue, it profeteth me nothynge.

Though I speake with the tongues of men & of Angels, and haue not charity I am become as sounding brasse or a tinkling cymbal.

2 And though I haue the gift of prophesie, and vnderstand all mysteries and all knowledge: and though I haue all faith, so that I could remooue mountaines, and haue no charitie, I am nothing.

3 And though I bestowe all my goods to feede the poore, and though I giue my body to bee burned, and haue not charitie, it profiteth me nothing.

Tyndale's Bible, 1528: I Corinthians, chapter 13, 1-3
Authorised Version, 1611: I Corinthians, chapter 13, 1-3

prose and ultimately in the Greek orators and Plato. The narrative prose of the Bible is at the delightful early stage represented also by Sir Thomas Malory or Berners' *Froissart*. Nothing could be more delightful in its own way than the manner of telling the stories in Genesis and the historical books generally, *e.g.* the story of the finding of Rebecca as a wife for Isaac : "And the servant took ten camels of the camels of his master and departed ; for all the goods of his master were in his hand : and he arose and went to Mesopotamia unto the city of Nahor. And he made his camels to kneel down without the city by a well of water at the time of the evening, even the time that women go out to draw water. And he said, O Lord God of my master Abraham, I pray thee, send me good speed this day, and shew kindness to my master Abraham. Behold I stand here by the well of water ; and the daughters of the men of the city come out to draw water : and let it come to pass, that the damsel to whom I shall say, Let down thy pitcher, I pray thee, that I may drink ; and she shall say, Drink, and I will give thy camels drink also ; let the same be she that thou hast appointed for thy servant Isaac ; and thereby shall I know that thou hast shewed kindness to my master. And it came to pass" etc.—and so it flows on with the successive "and," "and," "and." There is much worse narrative prose, but to write just so would be affectation though it has been used for translation of Homer. But the kind of prose which the English were learning in the sixteenth century had another origin. It was with their practice of dialectic that the Greeks learned and taught others the prose of exposition and demonstration. That is not the way of the East. The Oriental teacher imparts his intuitions to his pupils in brief sentences as in the *Book of Proverbs, Ecclesiastes* and even the Sermon on the Mount. St. Paul was learning a new dialectic, yet it is not difficult to note how he struggles to give the form of dialectic, demonstration, to his intuitions. No ; it is elsewhere than in the *form* of prose or verse that one must look for the influence of the Bible on our literature.

There is firstly the great background of story, characters, teachings, proverbs, parables, poetry, made familiar as their daily bread to the mass of the people. Of course all this does not come direct from the text of the Bible. Much of the Bible story had been made, as has been said above, familiar from the Miracle plays and other sources. But this was a strange medley of what was Biblical and what the fancy of the dramatiser had added to enliven the play. The mediaeval peasant had heard of Noah and his wife :

> Hastow not herd, quod Nicolas also,
> The sorwe of Noah with his felawshipe,
> Ere that he mighte gete his wife to ship ?
> Him had be lever, I dar wel undertake,

FIRST PAGE OF ST. MATTHEW'S GOSPEL

Fifteenth century illuminated MS. of the Wyclifite Bible

By courtesy of the University Library, Cambridge

BUNYAN'S COTTAGE, ELSTOW, BEDFORD

At thilke tyme, than alle his wethers blake,
That she had had a ship herself allone.

He knew of Herod and Pilate as notorious braggarts, and had pictured
to himself the shepherds of the Nativity as English peasants blowing
their nails on a cold night and complaining of landlords and tax-collectors.
With Shakespeare that is all changed. He is not a religious poet like
Milton, shaping to himself the story of man's fall as he accepts it from
the Scriptures, though Bishop Wordsworth has no difficulty, in his
interesting volume *Shakespeare and the Bible* (1880), in showing how
essentially Christian and Biblical are the sentiments his characters
give expression to throughout. In another chapter he shows that Shakespeare's use of Biblical stories, of Adam and Eve, Cain and Abel, Noah,
Jacob, Joseph, Jeptha, David and Goliath and so on are obviously known
to him from the Bible, so that he as often as not uses the very language
of the Scriptures. Occasionally Wordsworth falls into the not uncommon
error of attributing to Shakespeare's memory of the original what he has
got more shortly from Holinshed or other source. He also failed to notice
that the text with which Shakespeare was familiar is that of the Geneva
version. This has been much laboured of late, but one example is
conclusive proof. Discussing the speech of Shylock : "Yes to smell
pork ; to eat the habitation which your prophet the Nazarite conjured
the devil into," the Bishop asks : "Had our poet any reason for making
use of the name Nazarite rather than Nazarene . . . or was it a mistake ?"
If he had looked at the Genevan version of Matthew ii. 23, he would
have found that where the Authorised reads: "He shall be called a Nazarene," the Genevan Bible reads : "That hee should be called a Nazarite."

Of Shakespeare's effective use of Bible incidents it may suffice to cite
two instances : the application of the story of Jacob and the "eanlings
streak'd and pied" to the subject of interest on money in a spirit both
Biblical and Aristotelian, and the comment of Antonio, reminiscent of
the story of the Temptation :

The devil can cite Scripture for his purpose.
(*Merchant of Venice*)

Perhaps the most moving is the passionate speech of the forsaken Richard :

Give sorrow leave awhile to tutor me
To this submission. Yet I well remember
The favours of these men. Were they not mine ?
Did they not sometime cry "All hail" to me ?
As Judas did to Christ : but he in twelve
Found truth in all but one ; I in twelve thousand none.

. . . .

Nay all of you that stand and look upon,
Whilst that my wretchedness doth bait myself,

> Though some of you with Pilate wash your hands,
> Showing an outward pity ; yet you Pilates
> Have here delivered me to my sour cross,
> And water cannot wash away your sin.
>
> *(Richard II)*

Shakespeare may be taken for many others who in the course of our literature, not writing on devout themes, have found in Scriptural allusion and phrasing some of the most moving of their effects. For with the stories and wisdom and poetry came new words and effective phrases applicable to many circumstances. To Tyndale we owe, as has been said, the form Jehovah which we are now asked to abandon for the more barbaric-sounding Javeh. The late Henry Bradley, in that delightful book, *The Making of English*, attributes to him "long-suffering" and "peacemakers" (for "eirenopoioi"), and points out that the word "beautiful" has not been found used by any writer before Tyndale : "He certainly did not invent it, but there is no doubt that by introducing it into the People's Book he helped to bring it into general use." To Coverdale he attributes "lovingkindness" and "tender mercy." But besides words there are innumerable phrases which have become applicable beyond their first use : "A perfect Babel," "the Prophet's chamber," "the wise and foolish virgins," "to cast pearls before swine," "Gallio-like behaviour," "the eleventh hour" and many others. The whole tone of the Old and the New Testament is one of elevated and passionate sentiment that could not but quicken the imagination of a poet. There is not a great deal of purely picturesque and sensuous poetry, if there are some lovely passages. The "luscious" imagery of which Mr. Somerset Maugham complains is to be found in the *Song of Solomon*, both luscious and quaintly oriental: "Thy neck is as a tower of ivory; thine eyes like the fishpools in Heshbon by the gate of Bath-rabbim ; thy nose is as the tower of Lebanon which looketh toward Damascus." In the Apocalypse precious stones abound. Yet sensuousness is not the note of Biblical imagery. Even in the *Song* we get a more passionate strain : "Love is strong as death ; jealousy is cruel as the grave . . . Many waters cannot quench love." "Thou art beautiful, O my love, as Tirzah, comely as Jerusalem, terrible as an army with banners." "Until the day break, and the shadows flee away." Realism and passion are the note of Biblical imagery. It was to the Greek and Latin classics, especially Ovid, Virgil and Homer, that our poets went for sources of picturesque description such as one gets in the *Merchant of Venice* :

> The moon shines bright, in such a night as this,
> When the sweet wind did gently kiss the trees,
> And they did make no noise, in such a night
> Troilus methinks mounted the Troyan walls
> And sigh'd his soul toward the Grecian tents

NOAH'S ARK
Woodcut from Caxton's *Golden Legend*, 1483

Where Cressid lay that night. In such a night
Did Thisbe fearfully o'ertrip the dew . . .
                          In such a night
Stood Dido with a willow in her hand,

and so on in story after story from Ovid ; and Milton can write in the same vein :

This saying, from her husband's hand her hand
Soft she withdrew, and like a Woodnymph light
Oread or Dryad, or of Delia's train,
Betook her to the groves, but Delia's self
In gait surpass'd and Goddesslike deport.

There is little of that kind of painting in the Scriptures. The metaphors and hyperboles and personifications of Hebrew poetry breathe something of what Grote calls the terrible intensity of the Semitic mind, (the "ferocious strength of will") : "the mountains melted from before the Lord," "the stars in their courses fought against Sisera," "the beauty

of Israel is slain upon thy high places : how are the mighty fallen,"
"Saul and Jonathan were lovely and pleasant in their lives, and in their
death they were not divided : they were swifter than eagles, they were
stronger than lions," "woe unto them that draw iniquity with cords of
vanity, and sin as a cart-rope," "But the wicked are like a troubled sea,
for it cannot rest, and its waters cast up mire and dirt," "for he that
wavereth is like a wave of the sea driven with the wind and tossed,"
"they sow the wind and they shall reap the whirlwind," "As the shepherd
rescueth out of the mouth of the lion two legs or a piece of an ear so shall
they be rescued that sit in Samaria in the corner of a couch and on the
silken cushions of a bed" ; but there is no end to these sublime and
passionate figures. They are of the kind to which Shakespeare approxi-
mated in the great tragedies, *Hamlet, Macbeth, Othello, Lear*, and in some
of those gathered in Wolfgang Clemens' interesting study of Shakespeare's
imagery it seems to me that, consciously or half-consciously, the nucleus
of the figure has come to the dramatist from his memory of a Biblical
image : "The sun of Rome is set" (J.C. V. 3. 61) recalls "her sun
is gone down while yet day" (Jer. xv. 9); "conjures the wandering stars
and makes them stand" (Ham. V. i. 278), "Sun stand thou still upon
Gibeon, and thou Moon in the valley of Ajalon." (Josh. x. 12) ; "Life's
but a walking shadow" (Macb. V. v. 20), "Man that is born of woman
is of few days and full of trouble. He cometh forth like a flower and is
cut down ; he fleeth also as a shadow and continueth not." (Job. xiv. 1-2) ;
"His virtues will plead like angels trumpet-tongued against The deep
damnation of his taking off" (Macb. I. vii. 19), "And he shall send his
angels with a great sound of a trumpet, etc." (Matth. xxiv. 31) ; "for fear
the very stones prate of my whereabout" (Macb. II. i. 58), "The stones
shall cry out of the wall" (Hab. ii. 11). "A man . . . That thunders,
lightens, opens graves and roars" (J.C. I. iii. 72) is an obvious reference
to "and the earth did quake and the rocks rent, and the graves were opened"
(Matth. xxvii. 51-2). The long speech in Hamlet about "some vicious
mole," "some habit that too much o'er-leavens The form of plausive
manners, etc." is an elaboration of the text "A little leaven leaveneth the whole
lump," the thought of leaven as corrupting coming from the belief, expressed by Plutarch, concerning leaven, "itself the offspring of corruption
and corrupting the mass of dough."

If Shakespeare's metaphors seem at times to derive from the Bible,
and are of the same realistic, passionate kind, Milton in his last poems
more deliberately cultivated a style Biblical in its eschewing of decorative
writing. In *Paradise Lost* he had allowed himself a free use of the epic,
elaborate simile drawn in about equal measure from Nature, the Classics
and the Bible. In *Paradise Regained* there is not a single figure of this
kind in the first three books. In *Samson Agonistes* there is only one of a
decorative kind, and that in the ironical description of his wife :

That so bedeckt ornate and gay,
Comes this way sailing
Like a stately ship
Of Tarsus, bound for the Isles
Of Javan or Gadire
With all her bravery on, and tackle trim,
Sails fill'd, and streamers waving,
Courted by all the winds that hold them play,
An amber scent of odorous perfume
Her harbinger.

The few others are realistic and charged with feeling: "grow up and perish as the summer fly," "so much of adder's wisdom I have learned,"

Why are his gifts desirable : to tempt
Our earnest prayers, then given with solemn hand
As graces, draw a scorpion's tail behind ?

But Milton's deliberate use of the very words of Scripture requires and repays careful study. Underneath the classical cast of his sentence and verse lurks, or is obvious, a so exact use of the actual words that he is able to leave ambiguous the sense in which he himself understood them, which, as the *De Doctrina* shows, was not always the orthodox interpretation.

THE WORD OF GOD : MILTON TO RUSKIN

S has been said above, there are two things to be studied in estimating the effect of the Bible on English thought and literature—the translation regarded as a piece of literature, its influence on the diction and rhythm of our verse and prose, secondly, the Bible itself, accepted as the Word of God, superseding any claim of the Church as interpreter or as a vehicle of authoritative tradition. In the seventeenth century a great part of the English people, were, it has been said, "intoxicated with the poetry of the Bible and with the hope for a heaven on earth." In the great revival of the eighteenth century, Wesleyan and Evangelical, the influence of the Bible was still supreme, but its effect was softened and sentimentalized by what the earlier century had regarded with great suspicion, the appeal of hymns which were "merely human compositions." In the nineteenth century, cross-currents begin to flow.

29

To Milton the meeting of the Long Parliament, and opening of the Presbyterian attack upon the Prelates, was no merely political or even ecclesiastical event, it contained the hope of a Second Coming : "Come forth out of thy royal chambers, O Prince of all the Kings of the earth, put on the visible robes of thy imperial majesty, take up that unlimited sceptre which thy Almighty Father hath bequeathed thee ; for now the voice of thy Bride calls thee, and all creatures sigh to be renewed." In his controversy on the side of the Presbyterians Milton early became aware that the appeal to Antiquity, to history, was dangerous : "we both forsake our own grounds and reasons which led us at first to part from Rome, that is to hold the Scriptures against all antiquity ; we remove our cause into our adversaries' own court." The safest line for the Protestant is to allow no appeal from the Scripture : "Let them chant while they will of prerogatives, we shall tell them of Scripture ; of custom, we of Scripture ; of Acts and Statutes, still of Scripture, till the quick and piercing word enter to the dividing of their souls, and the mighty weakness of the Gospel throw down the weak mightiness of man's reasoning." "Wherefore should we not urge only the Gospel, and hold it ever in their faces like a mirror of diamond till it dazzle and pierce their misty eyeballs ? Maintaining it the honour of its absolute sufficiency and supremacy inviolable." Accordingly Milton set himself in the *De Doctrina Christiana* to work out for himself and "all Christians" a creed based on the Scriptures alone : "since I enroll myself among the number of those who acknowledge the Word of God alone as the rule of faith." "Let us then discard reason in sacred matters, and follow the doctrine of Holy Scripture exclusively." For the form of the great poem he was to make his life-work Milton chose as his models the classical poems of Greece and Rome ; for his critical guide "that sublime art which in Aristotle's Poetics, in Horace, and the Italian commentaries of Castelvetro, Tasso, Mazzini and others teaches what are the laws of a true epic poem, what of a dramatic, what of a lyric, what decorum is which is the grand masterpiece to observe." Yet even as early as this (1642) he finds in the Scriptures counterparts to each of these forms, and in lyrical poetry, "those frequent songs throughout the law and prophets . . . not in their divine argument alone, but in the very critical art of composition, may be easily made appear over all the kinds of lyrical poesy to be incomparable." Accordingly if *Paradise Lost* is a Virgilian epic, and *Samson Agonistes* a Sophoclean tragedy, *Paradise Regained* is modelled on the *Book of Job ;* and, in the final reply of the Saviour to Satan's eulogy of Athens, Milton finds in the Scriptures not only the fountainhead of truths unknown to the Greek Philosophers :

> Ignorant of themselves, of God much more,
> And how the world began, and how man fell
> Degraded by himself, on grace depending ;

JOHN MILTON, 1608-1674
Engraving by George Vertue

but he finds also poetic beauty and originality :

> Or if I would delight my private hours
> With music or with poem, where so soon
> As in our native language can I find
> That solace ? All our law and story strew'd
> With hymns, our psalms with artful terms inscrib'd,

31

Our Hebrew songs and harps in Babylon,
That pleas'd so well our victors' ear declare
That rather Greece from us these arts deriv'd.

In the *De Doctrina* Milton developed some heresies of his own. It cannot be said that even his Arianism intrudes itself obviously into the three poems in which he set forth the Christian doctrine of the Fall of Man, forfeiting or corrupting the divine gift of reason ; the Atonement by the perfect obedience and the death of the Son of God ; or thinking, if of himself also of the English people, the way of recovery ever open through repentance, "a broken and a contrite heart." But Milton's reading of Christian doctrine and experience was a stern one, emphasises the pessimistic strain which is not wanting in the Scriptures : "the regenerate are few," "Strait is the gate and narrow is the way, and few there be that find it," an aspect of Christian teaching which to the emotional convert, whose approach is more of the heart than of the intellect, is lost to sight in the entirety of his love and trust.

Such a more emotional approach was that of John Bunyan, for whom also the Bible was the sole and entire source of truth. His regard for the Bible made him as suspicious of the Quakers' "inner light" as of prelatical authority. In learning Bunyan was at the opposite pole from Milton, who read his Scriptures in the original Hebrew and Greek. The Latin translations in the *De Doctrina* are his own, certainly not those of the Vulgate ; Bunyan's quotations are from the Authorised version. In his *Grace Abounding to the Chief of Sinners*, where he describes the storms through which he passed between his first conviction of sin and the assurance of salvation, texts hum round his head like flies on a summer day, or like mosquitos on a damp evening, for they are as often alarming as consoling. They dart in through an open window, or sound in his ear like the voice that cried to Macbeth, "Sleep no more"—"now about a week or fortnight after this I was much followed by this Scripture, *Simon, Simon, behold Satan hath desired to have you*, Luke xxii. 31, and sometimes it would sound so loud within me, yea, as it were, call so strongly after me that once, above all, I turned my head over my shoulder thinking verily that some man had, behind me, called me being at a great distance methought he called so loud." And when, at length, assurance came to his tormented soul it was borne on the wings of a text : "Suddenly this sentence fell upon my soul, *Thy Righteousness is in Heaven ;* and methought withal, I saw with the eyes of my soul Jesus Christ at God's right hand, there, I saw, was my righteousness so that where ever I was, or whatever I was doing, God could not say of me *He wants my Righteousness*, for that was just before him." And so later Bunyan translated his experience, and the Scripture as he read it, into the well known allegory, *The Pilgrim's Progress*, in two parts, of Christian and of his wife Christiana, the marginal notes to which keep the reader in constant touch with the

'THE JUST UPRIGHT MAN IS LAUGHED TO SCORN'
Illustration to the *Book of Job*
Water colour by William Blake, 1757–1827
By courtesy of the Pierpont Morgan Library

LORD BYRON AS A BOY
Oil painting by Sir Thomas Lawrence, 1769–1830
By courtesy of the Leger Gallery, London

JOHN BUNYAN, 1628-1688
Drawing by Robert White

Scriptural authority. Thus four great imaginative works of the century, *Paradise Lost*, *Paradise Regained*, *Samson Agonistes* and *The Pilgrim's Progress* are the expression of a reaction intellectual and spiritual to the text of the Bible, read as the sole and complete word of God to men.

In the second great religious and puritan movement, of the following century, which is connected with the names of Watts, Whitefield, the Wesleys, Newton and Cowper, to say nothing of others, the Bible is once more the supreme revelation. The movement began, indeed, within the Church of England, at least as regards the Wesleys. In fact it was their regular, weekly attendance at the Eucharist which won for Charles and his small group of friends the title of "Methodists," before John had joined him at Oxford. It was this which evoked the scorn of their fellow-students, and the disapproval of the authorities. John Wesley had no desire to leave the Church, and had a regard for the history and authority of the Church. But this is not the place to sketch even in outline the history of Methodism. Wesley passed through a less agitated, but almost as painful, an experience as Bunyan before he found assurance of salvation,

33

through the influence of the Moravians, in the doctrine of the conviction of sin and acceptance of salvation through the merits and death of Christ, an experience which could be, and more often than not was, instantaneous, and was followed at once by the duty of preaching to others. His final conviction, and escape from the fear of death, which he had expressed to himself shortly before in the words of Donne :

> I have a sin of fear that when I have spun
> My last thread I shall perish on the shore,

was followed at once by the out-of-door preaching which, with the attendant phenomena of instantaneous conversion, was the great feature of Methodism. But if like Bunyan in this experience, he resembled Milton in another. He became gradually convinced that he had attached too much authority to Antiquity and Councils. In September 1713 he began reading over Bishop Beveridge's *Pandectae Canonum Conciliorum* (1672) and came to the conclusion that "Nothing could so effectually have convinced me that both particular and general councils may err, and have erred ; and of the infinite difference between the decisions of the wisest men and those of the Holy Ghost recorded in his word."

But the eighteenth was a less heroic, a more humanitarian, century than the seventeenth, and the most characteristic product of the Evangelical movement, whether without or later within the Church of England, was no Scriptural epic or allegory but a flood, one might almost say, of hymns. There had been much religious poetry in the former century, witness not Milton only but Donne, Herbert, Vaughan, Traherne and others ; but even the lyrical poems of such ardent souls were not hymns, not the expression of the Church, the Congregation, as such but of the individual mind and experience of the particular poet. The reason was, of course, the conviction of the Puritan, whether within or without the Church, that there must be no introduction into the service of the Church of merely human compositions, "adeoque nefas esse Christianorum aliquem ad ullum religionis cultusve actum cogi cuius ratio ex Scripturis reddi nequit aperta" (Ames : *Puritanismus Anglicanus*, 1658.) Our earliest post-Reformation hymns are the morning, evening and midnight hymns of Bishop Ken included in his *Manual of Prayers for Winchester Scholars* (1695). But our first great hymn-writer was Isaac Watts (1674-1748), whose earliest hymn was composed in the same year, 1695, "Behold the glories of the Lamb." He was not a Wesleyan but a Nonconformist minister in London. That he was aware of the innovation implied in the suggestion that hymns of "meer human composure" might be introduced into the worship of the Church is shown by the Preface to the *Hymns and Spiritual Songs* (1707) and by the title which he gave to his second volume, *The Psalms of David Imitated in the Language of the New Testament, and Apply'd to the Christian State and Worship* (1719). To

34

'CHRISTIAN MEETING EVANGELIST'
Illustration from Bunyan's *Pilgrim's Progress*, 1767 edition

this also is prefixed an *apologia* for his boldness, in which he claims that the Psalms of "the Royal Author" are not the fittest expression of the feelings of a Christian : "Moses, Deborah and the Princes of Israel and all the Saints under the Jewish State, sung their own Joys, and Victories, their own Hopes and Fears and Deliverances . . . and why must we, under the Gospel, sing nothing else but the Joys, Hopes and Fears of Asaph and David ? Why must Christians be forbidden all other Melody but what arises from the Victories and Deliverances of the Jews." "Some of them [the Psalms] are almost opposite to the spirit of the Gospel : Many of them foreign to the State of the New Testament, and widely different from the present circumstances of Christians . . . Thus by keeping too close to David in the House of God the Veil of Moses is thrown over our hearts." It is thus as a paraphrase of the first five verses of the ninetieth psalm that the best of his hymns, which might well replace any national anthem : "Our God, our help in ages past," appears in the 1719 volume. The other well-known hymn "When I survey the wondrous cross" belongs to the collection intended for use at the Communion service. The *Divine Songs Attempted in easy Language for the Use of Children* (1715) include some of a terrifying character :

> There is a dreadful Hell
> And everlasting pains
> Where sinners must with Devils dwell
> In darkness, fire and chains ;

but also the charming "Hush my Dear, lie still and slumber" and the once well-known " 'Tis the voice of the sluggard," "How doth the little busy bee," and "Let dogs delight to bark and bite." There was no thought in Watts's mind of disparaging the Scriptures : "I grant 'tis necessary and proper that in translating every Part of Scripture for our Reading or Hearing the Sense of the Original should be exactly and faithfully represented for there we hear what God says to us in his Word." But in singing it is *our* feelings that we are expressing, just as Asaph and "the Royal Author" had done.

Among the Wesleyans the best hymn-writer was Charles Wesley, though John made his contributions. To Charles we owe "Hark the Herald Angels sing," which in his own version ran "Hark through all the welkin rings," "Love divine all love excelling," "Lo he comes with clouds descending," "Christ the Lord is risen to-day," and others. The Wesleyans were in time divided into the Wesleyan Methodists and the Calvinist Methodists or Countess of Huntingdon's Connection. The leader of the Calvinists was the very emotional preacher Whitefield, John Wesley of the other division. But the most impassioned champion of Calvinism, Predestination, was not a Wesleyan but an evangelical minister in the Church of England, Augustus Toplady, a bitter opponent of John Wesley.

JOHN WESLEY PREACHING
Oil painting by P. J. de Loutherbourg, 1740-1812

It is in one of his impassioned defences of his doctrine that he bursts into his own great hymn, two verses of which express the quintessence of the Calvinist refusal of all merit except the imputed merits of Christ :

> Nothing in my hand I bring,
> Simply to thy cross I cling.

John and Charles Wesley, like Milton and Foxe earlier, rejected the doctrine but it was the faith of the two chief hymn writers of the Evangelical wing of the Church of England, Newton and Cowper. The *Olney Hymns* not infrequently, like those of Watts, refer to the text on which the hymn is based, *e.g.* "There is a fountain filled with blood" (Zech. xiii. 1.), "Hark my soul it is the Lord" (John xxi. 16.) But William Cowper has a larger interest than merely as the author of the above hymns as well as of "God moves in a mysterious way." He, in a way, linked Evangelical religion with the Nature poetry of the century which, influenced by Newton's discoveries, tended in Thomson's *Seasons*, towards a rhetorical Deism. In Cowper's poems the Methodist rejection of the world and its enticements and "laying up treasures on earth" readily blended with the invalid's love of retirement and of the country :

> God made the country and man made the town.

None of the landscape poets of the century came so near to the mood of Wordsworth as Cowper :

> Oh nature ! whose Elysian scenes disclose
> His bright perfections at whose word they rose,
> Next to that Power who form'd thee and sustains,
> Be thou the great inspirer of my strains.

In *A Winter Walk at Noon* in the *Task* Cowper anticipates a mood of Wordsworth :

> No noise is here, or none that hinders thought.
> The redbreast warbles still, but is content
> With slender notes, and more than half suppress'd :
> Pleas'd with his solitude, and flitting light
> From spray to spray, where'er he rests he shakes
> From many a twig the pendent drops of ice,
> That tinkle in the wither'd leaves below.
> Stillness accompanied with sounds so soft
> Charms more than silence. Meditation here
> May think down hours to moments. Here the heart
> May give an useful lesson to the head,
> And learning wiser grow without his books.

That is Wordworth's :

> Books ! 'tis a dull and endless strife :
> Come hear the woodland linnet !
> How sweet his music ! On my life,
> There's more of wisdom in it !

But Cowper will not go the whole way with Wordsworth. A retired life in contact with the beauties of Nature may produce a mood conducive to meditation and acceptance of the Truth. But to find that Truth, and a saving knowledge of God, one must go to a Book. The cottage wife may be wiser than Voltaire, for she :

> Just knows, and knows no more, her Bible true—
> A truth the brilliant Frenchman never knew,
> And in that charter reads with sparkling eyes
> Her title to a treasure in the skies.

Knowing his Bible Cowper knows that the geologists, who were later to trouble Tennyson, are just wrong :

> some drill and bore
> The solid earth, and from the strata there
> Extract a register, by which we learn

WILLIAM COWPER, 1731-1800
Pastel by George Romney, 1792

That He who made it and reveal'd its date
To Moses was mistaken in its age.

It was, a French historian tells us, the Evangelical influence which
more than anything else saved us from the horrors of the French Revolution.
Nor did the influence quickly pass away in the century which followed.
The definite teaching about Sin and Guilt, Heaven and Hell (not least the
latter), Conversion and Sanctification remained a power which, accepted

39

or rebelled against, formed a great part of the background of English feeling and habits. The Bible and Watts's hymns, including the *Divine Songs for Children*, were what, a recent writer says, "all right-minded parents" brought up their children on. So dominant was Evangelical Christianity that any definite attack, whether by a Paine or a Shelley, practically outlawed the writer here and, as Paine found, in America. To Lamb even, it seemed that Shelley's theories were "miching malice and mischief." To Charles Kingsley, Byron's poetry seemed less dangerous to a Christian than Shelley's. To an Evangelical like Richard Cargill, if we may trust Crabb Robinson, Wordsworth in the *Excursion* was anti-Christian : "It is only faith in the Redeemer that constitutes Christian feeling. Everything else is opposed to that." To another, Byron is much closer to the Christian truth : "He saw in his works the profoundest views of the depravity of human nature—not indeed spiritual views, but though not spiritually minded Lord Byron has described the human heart, and the intense truth of all his poetry is its great excellence." Byron, in fact, had been educated on the Bible in Calvinist Scotland and Methodist England, and he never outgrew the effect : "Send," he writes to Murray in 1821, "a common Bible, of a good legible print (bound in Russia). I *have* one ; but as it was the last gift of my Sister (whom I shall probably never see again) I can only use it carefully, and less frequently, because I like to keep it in good order. Don't forget this, for I am a great reader and admirer of those books, and had read them through before I was eight years old—that is to say, the *Old* Testament, for the New struck me as a task, but the other as a pleasure. I speak as a *boy*, from the recollected impression of that period at Aberdeen in 1796." Poor Fletcher's illiterate letter to Augusta tells how the convulsive attacks which led up to the final illness "Made, my Lord Doubley attentive Both to the Maxim of Low Living and the More Greater Duty of a good Christian which I am verry Happy to say My Lord Studyed most Fer-ventley for the Bible was Placed on his Lordship's Breakfast table has reagularly has his Simple Cup of tea which his Lordship always Drank with out either Cream or Suger." Augusta's gift and Fletcher's record are more characteristic of the period than significant as to Byron's mind. But indeed it needs no psychologist to discover what is written so clearly over all he composed. It is the Orthodox Evangelical doctrine of sin and guilt and retribution with which Byron is always inwardly at war :

> Our life is a false nature—'tis not in
> The harmony of things,—this hard decree,
> This ineradicable taint of sin,
> This boundless Upas,—this all-blasting tree,
> Whose root is earth—whose leaves and branches be
> The skies which rain their plagues on men like dew—

'ELIJAH RESTORING THE WIDOW'S SON'
Water colour by Ford Madox Brown, 1868
By courtesy of the Victoria & Albert Museum

JOHN RUSKIN 1819–1900
Water colour by Sir Hubert von Herkomer, 1881
By courtesy of the National Portrait Gallery

Disease, death, bondage—all the woes we see,
And worse, the woes we see not—which throb through
The immedicable soul, with heart-aches ever new.

"Of the Immortality of the Soul it appears to me that there can be little doubt. . . . A material resurrection seems strange, and even absurd, except for purposes of punishment ; and all punishment which is to revenge rather than to correct must be morally wrong. . . . Human passions have probably disfigured the divine doctrines here, but the whole thing is inscrutable. It is useless to tell me *not* to *reason* but to *believe*. You might as well tell a man not to wake but *sleep*. And then to *bully* with torments, and all that. I cannot help thinking that the *menace* of Hell makes as many devils as the severe penal codes of inhuman humanity make villains." "Man is born *passionate* of body, but with an innate though secret tendency to the love of Good in his Mainspring of Mind. But God help us all ! It is at present a sad jar of atoms." (*Detached Thoughts*). The motive running through Byron's tales and tragedies is clear. Good and evil in human nature are too strangely blended for pious judgements. All the heroes of his early melodramatic tales in verse are, or are meant to be, "great, bad men." It is the same with the more readable of the dramas. Sardanapalus is a voluptuary but courageous and humane. Cain is a noble if passionate creature. Cain's descendants, in *Heaven and Earth*, are superior to those who are content to live on when all their fellows are to perish, to live on to repeat the same sins and endure the same woes. "If the whole world were going to Hell," he told Kennedy, "he would prefer going with them." Southey's ridiculous poem provoked a rather scurrilous opening to the *Vision of Judgement*, but neither in that brilliant poem nor the greater *Don Juan* is Christianity treated with Voltairean levity. His last journey to Greece may, if one wishes, be regarded as a fresh bid for popularity; his motives were always mixed. A charitable mind would see in it, at least *also*, a desire to do something worthy before his death, even a note of penitence : "Poverty is wretchedness ; but it is perhaps to be preferred to the heartless, unmeaning dissipation of the higher orders. I am thankful I am now clear of that, and my resolution to remain clear of it for the rest of my life is immovable."

If Byron was the only one of the greater romantics whom Biblical, Evangelical Christianity had got *inside*, so that he might rebel but could never ignore or entirely reject, the Victorian whose work was shaped and coloured by the same influence, whether he wrote on painting and architecture or on economic and social problems, was John Ruskin. "Walter Scott and Pope's *Homer* were reading of my own election, but my mother forced me, by steady daily toil, to learn long chapters of the Bible by heart, as well as to read it every syllable through, aloud, hard names and all, from Genesis to the Apocalypse, about once a year : and to that discipline

—patient, accurate, and resolute—I owe, not only a knowledge of the Book, which I find occasionally serviceable, but much of my general power of taking pains, and the best part of my taste in literature. From Sir Walter Scott's novels I might easily, as I grew older, have fallen to other people's novels ; and Pope might, perhaps, have led me to take Johnson's English, or Gibbon's, as types of language ; but once knowing the 32nd of Deuteronomy, the 119th Psalm, the 15th of 1st Corinthians, the Sermon on the Mount, and most of the Apocalypse, every syllable by heart, and having always a way of thinking with myself what words meant, it was not possible for me, even in the foolishest times of youth, to write entirely superficial or formal English ; and the affectation of trying to write like Hooker and George Herbert was the most innocent I could have fallen into." (*Praeterita*). But it was not only to know good English prose from less good that Ruskin learned from this extraordinary (surely even in those days) idolatry of the Bible. It was much more. His mother had " 'devoted me to God' before I was born ; in imitation of Hannah . . . Devoting me to God meant, as far as my mother knew herself what she meant, that she would try to send me to college and make a clergyman of me ; and I was accordingly bred for the Church." While a small child he preaches to his mother and her friends, "the sermon some eleven words long . . . and I still think must have been the purest gospel, for I know it began 'People, be good.' " Once begun Ruskin was never to cease preaching, and on the theme that people must be good if they are to do any good work, that all good art and architecture must have been the work of good men, of good social conditions. And "good" Ruskin understood in the narrow Evangelical sense of the word : "All my first books, to the end of the *Stones of Venice*, were written in the simple belief I had been taught as a child." In *Modern Painters* his praise of Turner for the truth of his representation of nature, and his own minute studies of different aspects of trees, rocks and mountains, are in the spirit of Cowper, and the objective style of Scott, rather than in the pantheistic mood of Wordsworth. And texts come almost as readily to his mind as to Bunyan's. The General Index to that work alone shows some two hundred and fifty references, and those from Genesis to Micah in the Old Testament and from Matthew to the Apocalypse in the New. His works on architecture were inspired by the same religious spirit : "In all my past work, my endeavour has been to show that good architecture is essentially religious—the production of a faithful and virtuous not an infidel and corrupted people. But I have had also to show that good architecture is not ecclesiastical . . . Good architecture has always been the work of the commonality, not the clergy . . It is the manly language of a people inspired by resolute and common purpose, and rendering resolute and common fidelity to the legible laws of an undoubted God." (*Crown of Wild Olives*.) If Ruskin gradually fell away from his Evangelical

'THE SLUGGARD'
Engraving by H. Fitzcook
Illustration to Watts's *Divine and Moral Songs for Children*

religion, the religion of conversion and salvation by faith, it was in the main because he felt so acutely the interval between Christian teaching, the Sermon on the Mount, and Christian Capitalist society. But that did not alter the Christian spirit of his work nor his use of the Bible : *Unto This Last* (1860), his first "heretical" work, owes its title and tenor to the Gospels. If his interest in the Bible altered it was, as with many others, that it shifts from the Law to the Prophets in the Old Testament, from the Epistles of St. Paul, who to Bunyan was "one of a thousand ; he can beget Children, travel in Birth with Children, and nurse them himself when they are born" (*Pilgrim's Progress*), to the more practical Catholic Epistles, which Luther despised but which, Ruskin tells the workmen of Sheffield "are written to you . . as much as anyone else— the Pauline epistles being only to special persons. . . . But the Catholic epistles are directly addressed to you—every word vital for you; and the most vital of these is the one that is given in nearly the same words by two of the Apostles, Peter and Judas (not Iscariot) namely 2 Peter i. 19, to end of epistle and the epistle of Jude entire . . . For if you understand those two epistles . . . you will also understand the definition of true religious service by St. James the Bishop . . . to wit 'Pure service and undefiled . . . before God and the Father is this, to visit the fatherless and widows in their affliction, and to keep himself unspotted from the world.'"

The falling away of Ruskin from the Evangelical, Biblical religion in which he had been educated, and in which he had set out to preach and to open the eyes of readers to the moral and spiritual significance of art, is symptomatic of what I have called the cross-currents which in the century began to flow. On the one hand was the reversion to the authority of the Church in Christian teaching and order, represented among other symptoms by the Oxford Movement of the middle of the century, a move- ment, which, like the Methodist revival a century before, was the effect of a reaction against the increasing secularity of political and social life, but also of a growing suspicion, quickened by the reports blowing in from the country of Luther, that the Bible itself was not to remain exempt from criticism. The second current was just this of criticism, the appli- cation to the Scriptures of the same critical spirit as had been applied to the poems of Homer and other writings come down from antiquity. It is not my intention to enter at length on either of these. For thousands of people, here and in America and the Dominions, the Bible remained and remains the Word of God much as it was to Milton and Bunyan. What the Bible, read as the Word of God, in the last three centuries has been to the British people has been well stated by a Catholic : "Who will not say that the uncommon beauty and marvellous English of the Pro- testant Bible is not one of the great strongholds of heresy in this country ? It lives on the ear like music that can never be forgotten—like the sound of a church-bell which a convert hardly knows he can forgo. . . It is part

of the national mind and the anchor of national seriousness. The memory of the dead passes into it. The potent traditions of childhood are stereotyped in its verses. The dower of all the gifts and trials of a man's life is hidden beneath its words. It is the representative of the best moments ; and all that there has been about him of soft and gentle, and pure and penitent and good, speaks to him for ever out of the English Bible. It is his sacred thing which doubt has never dimmed and controversy never soiled. [Here, in quoting, Ruskin interjects "Doctor ! " for certainly there has been much controversy, and Christians have spoken of Christians in language which is a disgrace to humanity.] In the length and breadth of the land there is not a Protestant with a spark of righteousness about him whose spiritual biography is not his English Bible." (Faber, quoted in Ruskin's *Fors Clavigera*. Letter LXXVI. Notes.)

Moreover, if criticism has for some, perhaps many, people robbed the Bible of some of what might be called the magical character it had for those whom we have had in view, the feeling that could make even a man like John Wesley seek guidance from a casual opening of the book, it has for many others by no means weakened its religious value and appeal. It has rather, by showing the various constituents of the Book in better perspective, made it easier, in the words of a great critic: "to separate dead tradition from living truth and to feel a Spirit not their own working through and upon the ancestral institutions and practices of Israel, upon tribal and local ideas of God . . . lifting up and transforming these to a degree which justifies the divine claim, *Behold I make all things new*." (George Adam Smith : *Teaching of the Old Testament in Schools*.) Of one aspect of the new perspective the interest and importance for to-day may excuse a few words. I have already come near to it in speaking of the swing over of Ruskin from the Evangelical concentration on the

45

individual's conversion and salvation by faith to the demand for a Christian economic and social reform. As a consequence of the new criticism, says the writer quoted above, "in particular the prophets came to their own with us." The swing over has been stated more strongly by the late C. J. Montefiore : "To our forefathers, Amos, Hosea and Isaiah were all later than the Law in time and inferior in greatness and authority . . . to us they are earlier in time and superior in greatness and authority." The prophets had been studied in the centuries on which I have touched (I speak subject to some correction, there were doubtless exceptions) mainly to trace the predictions of the Messiah, and of the future, as far as might be, of the Church and the World. What had been in great measure overlooked was their social implications, the significance of the cry of Amos and Micah and Isaiah : "I hate, I despise your feastdays, and I will not smell in your solemn assemblies. Though ye offer me burnt offerings and your meat offerings, I will not accept them . . . Take thou away from me the noise of thy songs ; for I will not hear the melody of thy viols. But let judgement run down as waters, and righteousness as a mighty stream." (Amos v. 21-4.) "Will the Lord be pleased with thousands of rams or with ten thousands of rivers of oil ? Shall I give my firstborn for my transgression, the fruit of my body for the sin of my soul ? He hath showed thee, O man, what is good ; and what doth the Lord require of thee, but to do justly and to love mercy, and to walk humbly with thy God." (Micah vi. 7, 8.) It was in just such a spirit that Ruskin made up his mind that it was not for him enough to be pious and to subscribe largely to charities at home or abroad, but that the first duty of a Christian was to work for the reconstruction of society on a basis of justice and mercy : "For my own part I will put up with this state of things passively not an hour longer. I am not an unselfish person, nor an Evangelical one ; I have no particular pleasure in doing good ; neither do I dislike doing it so much as to expect to be rewarded for it in another world. But I simply cannot paint, nor read, nor look at minerals, nor do anything else that I like, and the very light of the morning sky, when there is any—which is seldom now-a-days near London—has become hateful to me, because of the misery that I know of, and see signs of, where I know it not, which no imagination can interpret too bitterly." (*Fors Clavigera*, Letter I.) That the same revolutionary spirit lurked in the Prophets was so little suspected that poor Tom Paine could abuse the prophets in *The Age of Reason* without a suspicion that they had been fighting in their day the same battle as himself, against the exploitation of the poor by the rich : "Woe unto them that join house to house, that lay field to field, till there be no room, and ye be made to dwell alone in the midst of the land." "Woe unto them that decree unrighteous decrees, and to the writers that write perverseness : to turn aside the needy from judgement, and to take away the right of the poor of my

".... To whom thus Adam called
'Haste hither, Eve, and worth thy sight behold
Eastward among those trees, what glorious shape
Comes this way moving . . . .'"

Illustration to Milton's *PARADISE LOST* by John Martin, 1827

people, that widows may be their spoil, and that they may make the father-less their prey ! " But I need not accumulate instances. The protest of Ruskin against the doctrine of *laisser faire*, that doctrine of "liberty in the interests of the employing and commercial classes" (Nietsche), aroused so much outcry that the editor of the *Cornhill Magazine* had to discontinue the publication of his *Unto This Last,* and the publishers of *Fraser's Magazine* had to compel the editor to do likewise with the essays which became *Munera Pulveris.* "Only a genius like Mr. Ruskin could have produced such hopeless rubbish" was one line of criticism, but the rubbish was also alarming. If to-day we hear Ruskin's condemnation of a purely profiteering industry echoed from every side, from Archbishops to the humbler clergy, it is a compliment to Ruskin. But it is more. It is a proof that, if in different senses to different people and times, the Bible has proved itself the word of God in its unfailing witness to the demands of justice and mercy. "I am thankful," wrote a Scottish divine to Carlyle, apropos of Ruskin's articles, "for any unveiling of the so-called science of political economy, according to which avowed selfishness is the rule

47

of the world. It is indeed most important preaching—to preach that there is not one God for religion and another God for human fellowship—and another God for buying and selling—that pestilent polytheism has been largely and confidently preached in our time, and blessed are those who can detect its mendacities, and help to disenchant the brethren of their power." "Let not the wise man glory in his wisdom, neither let the mighty man glory in his might, let not the rich man glory in his riches : but let him that glorieth glory in this, that he understandeth that I am the Lord which exercise lovingkindness, judgement, and righteousness in the earth: for in these things I delight, saith the Lord." (Jeremiah ix. 23-5.)

"In assuming that the English Bible may yet be made the rule of faith and conduct," wrote Ruskin, long after he had abandoned the faith of his early training, "much more is of course accepted as the basis of our future education than the reader will find taken for granted in any of my writings on political economy previous to the year 1875. It may partly account for the want of success of those writings that they pleaded for honesty without praise, and for charity without reward ;—that they entirely rejected, as any motive of moral action, the fear of future judgement ; and—taking St. Paul in his irony at his bitterest word,—*Let us eat and drink, for to-morrow we die*, they merely expanded that worldly resolution into its just terms : Yes, let us eat and drink—what else ? but let us *all* eat and drink, and not a few only, enjoining fast to the rest." (*Fors Clavigera*, Letter LXXXVI).